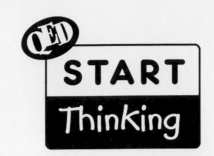

Keeping Healthy

Sally Hewitt

QED Publishing

First published in the UK in 2005 by
QED Publishing
A Quarto Group company
226 City Road
London EC1V 2TT
www.qed-publishing.co.uk

A Catalogue record for this book is available from the British Library.

ISBN 1 84538 159 9

Written by Sally Hewitt
Designed by Caroline Grimshaw
Editor Hannah Ray
Picture Researcher Nic Dean

Series Consultant Anne Faundez
Publisher Steve Evans
Creative Director Louise Morley
Editorial Manager Jean Coppendale

Printed and bound in China

Picture credits

Key: t = top, b = bottom, m = middle, l = left, r = right

Corbis/LWA-Dann Tardif 4b, / Ariel Skelley 5, 18l, /Richard Cummins 6,
/Hughes Martin 9, /Tom Stewart 13, 20r, /Garie Hind 14, /JLP/Jose L. Pelaez
16, 21l, /FK Photo 17, / Jose Luis Pelaez, Inc. 22b; **Getty Images**/Camille
Tokerud/The Image Bank 7r, 18r, /John-Francis Bourke/The Image Bank 7l,
/Julian Calder/Stone 10, 19l, /Ross Whitaker/The Image Bank 11,/James
Darell/Stone 12, 20l.

Contents

Your body

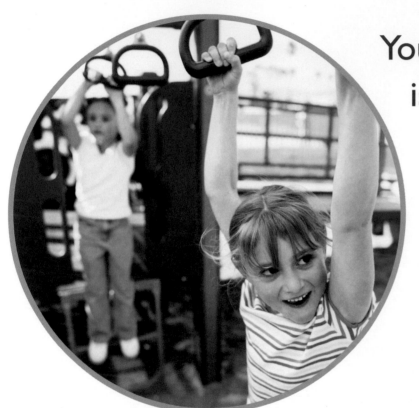

Your body
is amazing.
It can think
and learn, run
and play.

It can see, hear,
smell, taste and feel.

There are lots of
things you can do to
help your body to
grow, and to keep it
strong and **healthy**.

5

Eat well

You need **energy** for everything you do.

Food and drink give you energy. If you don't eat or drink enough, you will soon feel tired.

When you feel hungry,
eat fresh food and
plenty of fruit
and vegetables.

When you feel thirsty,
drink milk, juice and
plenty of water.

Keep moving

Moving makes your body work harder.

It makes your **heart** pump faster and your lungs breathe in more air.

Moving helps to keep your muscles and bones strong.

You can walk, run, climb and swim.
You can play sport and games.
Moving can be fun!

Fight germs

Tiny germs, too small to see, can make you feel ill.

When you feel unwell, keeping warm and resting helps your body to fight germs and to get better.

10

Germs can get on your hands.
Make sure that you wash
your hands before you eat.

Sunshine and fresh air help
to keep you healthy.

Hot sun can burn your skin,
so wear sun cream and a hat.

When it's
cold outside,
wrap up
warm
and have
something
hot to eat
and drink.

Getting too
cold makes
you shiver!

Keep clean

During the day you might get hot and sweaty, and covered in dirt.

A bath or shower washes away germs and keeps you smelling sweet!

Germs stick
to your teeth when
you eat and drink.

Brush your teeth
every morning and
every evening to get
rid of germs, and
to keep your smile
shiny and bright.

15

After a busy day, your body needs a **rest**. It has been thinking, moving and working very hard.

While you are asleep, your body has a long rest.

16

You need plenty
of sleep to keep
you healthy.

When you wake
up, you are ready
for a new day.

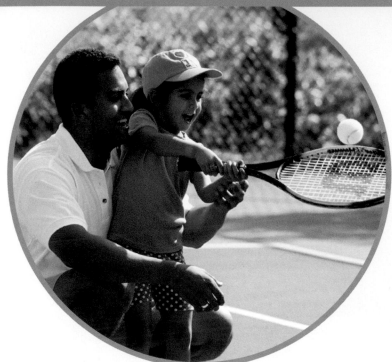

Can you remember some of the things that your amazing body can do?

What gives your body the energy it needs?

18

What do you like to do to keep your body moving?

How can you help your body to fight germs?

What can you do to keep safe in the hot sun?

What can you do to keep warm on a cold day?

20

Why should you brush
your teeth twice a day?

Why don't you stay
awake all day and
all night?

Energy – energy gives your body power to move and work.

Healthy – you are healthy when you are strong and fit and well.

Heart – your heart pumps blood all round your body. Exercise helps to keep your heart healthy.

Rest – your body rests while you are asleep. Without rest, you feel very tired.

Index

Parents' and teachers' notes

- Look at the cover of the book. Talk about the picture and why it has been chosen for the cover.
- Read the title of the book together. Explain that the title gives the reader an idea as to what the book is going to be about.
- Explain that this is a non-fiction book, which gives the reader facts and information. Talk about the differences between fiction, which is a story, and non-fiction.
- Read the book together, discussing the photographs as you read each page. What extra information do the photographs give the reader?
- Spend time talking together about the answers to the questions on pages 18–21. Look back through the book to find the answers.
- Identify the contents page, the glossary and the index.
- Using the contents page, look up the page entitled 'Keep moving'.
- Point out that the index is in alphabetical order. Explain that the index tells us where in the book we can find certain information. Use the index to look up the references to 'energy'.
- Find the words in **bold** type and look them up in the glossary.
- Discuss how you feel when you are healthy. Then ask your child if he or she can remember being ill. Can he or she remember how he or she felt?
- Make a healthy meal together and discuss why the food you have chosen is good for you.
- Together, make a list of things you enjoy doing that get you moving, e.g. swimming, going on bike rides.
- Help your child to find a pulse in his or her wrist or neck. Talk about how your heart beats faster after exercise.
- Look through the book and discuss what you do to keep healthy. Talk about what you could do to be even healthier.